How the B Got Its Stink

Written by
Jeanne Willis

Illustrated by
Tony Ross

OXFORD
UNIVERSITY PRESS

OXFORD
UNIVERSITY PRESS

Great Clarendon Street, Oxford, OX2 6DP, United Kingdom

Oxford University Press is a department of the University of Oxford.
It furthers the University's objective of excellence in research, scholarship,
and education by publishing worldwide. Oxford is a registered trade mark
of Oxford University Press in the UK and in certain other countries

British Library Cataloguing in Publication Data
Data available

ISBN: 978-0-19-835639-4

10 9 8 7 6 5 4

Paper used in the production of this book is a natural, recyclable product
made from wood grown in sustainable forests. The manufacturing process
conforms to the environmental regulations of the country of origin.

Printed in China by Leo Paper Products Ltd

Acknowledgements

Series Advisor: Nikki Gamble

Once, there was a family of Binks.
There was Father Bink,
Mother Bink,
Sister Bink
and Brother Bink.

They were the only Binks left in the woods.
Mother Bink was about to have twins.

But *something* was out to get them.

The Binks were very sweet and soft.
They were too sweet and too soft
for their own good.

They had no teeth to bite with.

And no claws to fight with.

One day, Sister Bink met a Snappy Fang.
"Hello, good to meet you!" said Sister Bink.

"Good to eat you!" said the Snappy Fang.
And he gobbled her up.

"Yum! So soft, so sweet!" said the Snappy Fang.
"Binks are easy to eat.
No teeth to bite me and no claws to fight me."

When Sister Bink did not come home,
Brother Bink went to look for her.

On the way, he met the Snappy Fang.
"Hello, good to meet you," said Brother Bink.

"Good to eat you!" said the Snappy Fang.

And he gobbled up Brother Bink.

Gobble!
Gobble!

"Yum. So soft,
so sweet!" he said.

"Binks are easy to eat.

No teeth to bite me and no claws to fight me.

But I am still hungry!"

So he hid and he waited.

Father Bink went to look for his children.
The Snappy Fang saw him and jumped out.

"Hello," said Father Bink.
"Good to meet you!"

"Good to eat you!" said the Snappy Fang.

And he gobbled up Father Bink.

Gobble!
Gobble!

"Yum. So soft, so sweet!" he said.

"Binks are easy to eat.

No teeth to bite me and no claws to fight me.

I will catch another one!" said the Snappy Fang.

He hid and he waited.

Father Bink, Brother Bink and Sister Bink
had not come home.

"Where are they?" said Mother Bink.

There was a knock at the door.

But it was not them.

It was the Wise Old Woodman. He had seen
the Snappy Fang eat the Binks and he was sad.
Soon there would be no Binks left in the woods.

"Mother Bink, I cannot make you less soft or sweet," said the Wise Old Woodman.

"I cannot give you teeth to bite or claws to fight. But I do have a way to save you and your babies, when they are born."

He made a special stinky cream and gave it to Mother Bink.

"That will do the trick," he said.

Mother Bink put it on her fur.

Squirt, squirt!

The next day, Mother Bink had her baby twins.
She put the cream on their fur, and she took
them out to show them off.

When the Snappy Fang saw them, he licked his lips. "Yum! *Three* Binks!" he said. "One for breakfast, one for lunch and one for tea!"

And he jumped out.

Rarrrrrrr!

"Hello, do you want to meet my babies?" said Mother Bink.

"I want to **eat** your babies!" said the Snappy Fang.

But as the Snappy Fang looked into the pram …

... he smelled the **stinkiest** stink that ever stunk.

"Yuck! Binks are smelly!
I don't want them in my belly!" said the Snappy Fang.
"I would rather starve than eat one."

He hiccupped and out came all the Binks!

That is why there are still Binks in the woods.

And that is how they got their stink!